Buildings for Best Products
The Museum of Modern Art, New York

Buildings for Best Products

The Museum of Modern Art, New York

Copyright © 1979 by The Museum of Modern Art
All rights reserved
ISBN 0-87070-239-4
Designed by Barbara Balch
Typeset by M.J. Baumwell Typography, Inc., New York, N.Y.
Printed by The Arts Publisher, Inc., Richmond, Va./New York, N.Y.
Bound by Sendor Bindery, Inc., New York, N.Y.
The Museum of Modern Art
11 West 53 Street, New York, N.Y. 10019
Printed in the United States of America

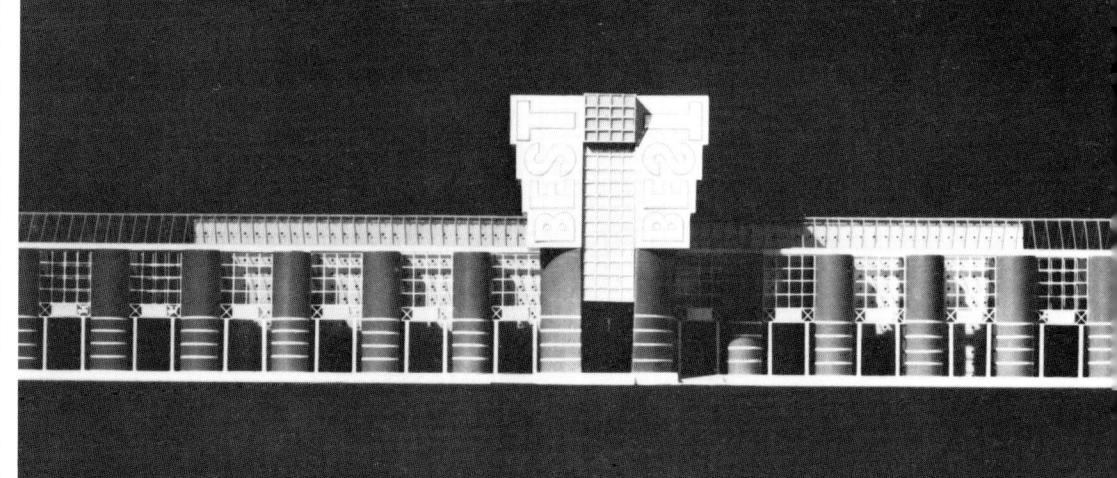

Foreword
Philip Johnson

Comparisons may be odious, but how is one to avoid them in discussing these disparate designs all aimed at decorating a "shed" — the Best Products Company standard box. The company is famous in architectural circles for the amazing designs by James Wines and SITE, which make a hard act to follow. Six of the bravest of the middle generation ("kids" to my generation) were selected by the Museum to participate.

The designs differ wildly and amusingly. I set up categories here more to make it easier to discuss their differences than because the categories are stringent. We have, accordingly, two witty comments, by Stern and Tigerman; two very serious stoas — Greek market arcades, the most time-honored shopping theme in our classical tradition — by Greenberg and Graves; two sculptural proposals — almost nonarchitectural — one serious by Tony Lumsden, one playful by Charles Moore.

Stern's Greek temple front is full of delightful jokes on classical architecture, on Vincent Scully, on consumers, jokes that improve on reading their explanations in Stern's equally witty prose. "Complexities and contradictions" abound. Violent scale shifts, outrageous "pop" allusions, a clashing color scheme — all tickle the fancy and arouse curiosity. If the ugly word postmodernism has any content, this is it. It will be fun to shop there.

Tigerman has a different kind of fun: the glorification of the split-level Colonial ranch house. But aside from the obvious "épater"-ing of the bourgeoisie (which the bourgeois will love) is the play of gigantism. We are all children; we love Alice when she eats the wrong (or right) side of the mushroom. Will it be exciting or confusing to enter under the broken garage door or both? Tigerman's cottage should have more impact than even the notorious Long Island "duck" of Venturi fame or a Hollywood Donut stand.

Our two serious stoas are miles apart in concept: Greenberg's, a meticulous working of the classical portico; Graves's, a contemporary version.

Greenberg has not worried about the scale of the original box. He creates a Tuscan-columned entryway scaled down to the human pedestrian approach to the front door. But what a front door! A round arch with architrave so broken, so tortured, that one can only rejoice at the smart originality. The side entrance and the main door have entablatures that would make 16th-century Manerists envious — or make them blush. Also, unlike the other architects, Greenberg is proposing lush marbles, fine unmodern materials, with which to amaze the visitor and to contrast with the plain-Jane wall behind.

Graves, on the contrary, scales his stoa to the height of the building, making a colossal porch for giant visitors. His drum columns are only reminiscences of the classical; his niched square piers are a new kind of pilaster. His roof is glass, not solid. The contrasting colonnettes — shades of Michelangelo's Campidoglio — support a vine-clad lattice, bringing the scale once again from the colossal to the human. The split and stepped keystone entry tower is a very Gravesian, a very original, very large symbolic eye-catcher that should prove very Bestian.

Our two sculptors can be considered separately. Lumsden is an intensive student of romantically curved glass sheets. He is, in addition, a very practical architect, working in a huge firm of architects. His artful proposal is more like the SITE solutions, and yet it too is a porte cochère in effect. A porte cochère of waving (as in ocean waves) glass that stabs through the facade of the building, "destroying" the facade yet emphasizing it. Hard to judge in the model, the overwhelming force of this design makes it the most startling of all.

Charles Moore — the sly fox — with his always brilliant collaborators, has opted for pure sculpture fun and games. The porcelain-enamel or specular-sheet-metal shapes glitter and shimmer like an Expressionist or Futurist dream pile. It is only with close inspection that the "mess" is seen as actually a group of elephants, seemingly full-scale, that the visitor passes through on his way to the doorways of the building hidden behind. If we are all still children, we shall marvel at the shimmering mirrors and enjoy the confusion of all the great elephants.

One wonders, looking at these designs: Where are we in the development of modern architecture? Nowhere, we are tempted to answer. Some directions: Startling shifts in the building fabric and scale à la Wines exemplified by Lumsden and Tigerman. Some historical allusions: Stern, Greenberg, and Graves. Some prefer pop: Tigerman, Moore. Some up-scaled sculpture — almost antiarchitectural: Lumsden. No International Style influence from the 30s, 40s, 50s, or 60s is observable. The Modern Movement seems really gone from the scene. But not modern architecture. Modern can still include Venturi; Hardy, Holzman, Pfeiffer; Wines — as well as our six. Harder to define than the International Style, less arrogant and self-satisfied with their moral superiority than their ancestors, architects today are more inclusive, more permissive, more popular-oriented, indeed more popular, than the Modern Movement allowed.

The most exciting part of the story is to come. What happens next?

Introduction
Arthur Drexler

The Best Products Company is a catalog-showroom merchandiser—by now the largest in the country. Its showrooms (they are not called stores) are located in shopping centers or on commercial strips. Customers drive out, choose what they want from samples on display, fill out an order form and hand it to a clerk, and collect their purchases at a counter convenient to the parking lot. The system is fast, efficient, and operates without a large sales staff.

As of 1979 Best Products has 74 showrooms in 10 states, of which half are in the "sunbelt," and has been adding 10 to 15 new showrooms each year. Whether or not they have ever visited a Best showroom, most architects and a large part of the public have heard about the company, because in 1972 it began to build a series of startling designs by an architectural group called SITE.

To this continuing series Best has recently added a showroom designed by Venturi and Rauch and an administration headquarters by Hardy Holzman Pfeiffer. Now, at the suggestion of Philip Johnson and in collaboration with The Museum of Modern Art, Best has asked six more architects to address the problem: What do you do with a showroom building that is essentially a windowless box? Their proposals, together with their own comments, appear on pages 22 through 45.

The standard Best Products building is a two-story brick-walled structure 203' wide, 190' deep, and 30' high. About 65 percent of its floor area functions as warehouse; the remainder is showroom. Internal arrangements have been refined over the years and are largely exempt from architectural innovations. The exterior, however, is another matter. It is a brick box with a canopy and a sign. Compared with the more aggressive varieties of commercial building its bland elevation is innocuous. It isn't "bad"; it isn't "good."

Much of the novelty of SITE's work has been that it avoids arguments about what is architecturally good or bad. In fact it seems to avoid architecture, concentrating instead on a sort of built commentary that starts with the original standard design and, by implication, takes on commercial building, the consumer society, the uses of ambiguity, and the relation of architecture to art. Considering that all this has been occasioned by the manipulation of facades, it is no small achievement.

SITE's first project for Best, in 1972, was not a new building but simply an alteration of an existing one. SITE added a veneer of brick to make a wall that looks as if it is peeling away from the building. This modest intervention removes the building from the realm of anonymity without introducing questions

*Above: Standard Best Products Showroom.
Opposite: SITE, Architects. Peeling Showroom, 1972. Richmond, Virginia.*

of architectural design. Instead it undermines the logic of the building —any building—with a modification that implies ultimate destruction.

The next project, a showroom in Houston completed in 1974, was rather more drastic. James Wines, one of the principals of SITE, describes the concept involved as "the 'de-architecturization' of the facade and side walls. This has been achieved by extending the brick veneer arbitrarily beyond the logical edge of the roofline, resulting in the appearance of architecture somewhere between construction and demolition. To intensify this ambiguity, a section of the central facade has been fragmented and the waste bricks allowed to spill over the top of the pedestrian canopy. Architecture is regarded, in the Houston project, as a matrix for art ideas and as a 'found object'—or the 'subject matter' for art, rather than the objective of design. The building also uses architecture as a means of social and psychological commentary, as opposed to an exploration of form, space, and structure."

Collapse and decay as architectural motifs have ample precedent. But this version differs markedly from sham Gothic or Roman ruins set down in pastoral landscapes for those who wish to brood on the vanity of earthly splendors. The Houston showroom's environment is not exactly pastoral, and the building's apparently ruinous state pertains not to a world long gone but to our own—giving a slightly different twist to the phrase "business as usual."

A 1977 project in Sacramento, California, called the Notch showroom, continued SITE's use of fragmentation and subtraction. As James Wines describes it: "The basic showroom prototype remains unchanged—again using architecture as the 'subject matter' or raw material of art, rather than the objective of a design process. However, whereas the 'indeterminate facade' uses additions as reductions, the 'Notch' showroom uses reductions as additions. In this case the building is penetrated by a 14' high raw-edged notch which serves as a main entranceway. The 45-ton wedge extracted from this gap is mounted on a rail system incised into the paving and mechanized to move a distance of 40' to open and close the showroom." Understandably, crowds of spectators assemble to watch the morning opening and evening closing.

Notch was followed by Tilt, built at Eudowood Mall in Towson, Maryland, in 1978. Where the first three projects described use the idea of disintegration, the fourth involves a more immediately apparent act of the will, and seems to center on the idea of incompletion, in that the

Above and opposite: SITE, Architects. Indeterminate Facade Showroom, 1975. Almeda-Genoa Shopping Center, Houston, Texas.

building is not broken but only in disarray. As Wines describes it: "The Tilt showroom is an inversion of the standard shopping-center structure and the architectural traditions of formalism and equilibrium. Its facade is a casually tilted plane made of masonry block, developed as a response to already existing physical and psychological circumstances. The Eudowood Mall site is a U-shaped retail center composed of rigidly vertical and horizontal elements, and the injection of this tilted wall establishes a visual dialogue between the routine utility of the Mall and the precariousness of the facade. The building is also a commentary on modern architecture's obsession with form as an expression of function. In this case, the function is not 'expressed,' but simply 'revealed' by lifting up one corner of the usual impediment between outside and inside."

Inevitably the viewer wonders whether the wall is safely secured; whether it can be set back in the right place; or whether it can be moved away. Architects may be reminded of orthodox modernism's preference for volumes defined by thin white planes that look as if they might be made of cardboard; architectural students may be reminded of a cardboard model dropped on the floor.

All of these SITE buildings, as well as others built and unbuilt, are jokes played on architecture (and only incidentally on the public). A more recent project, however, suggests a slight shift of interest. In 1978 SITE designed what it calls a Terrarium showroom for a mountainous site south of San Francisco. The intention was to pile earth on a stepped roof so that it would look like a segment of the surrounding landscape. A transparent skin of glass set 8" from the building's masonry wall was to have been filled with earth and rock approximating the actual strata of the area, and the roof was to have been covered with regional vegetation.

This ambitious project has not been built, but a much-simplified version, using only one wall of earth and rocks behind glass, is now under construction in Hialeah, Florida. In both versions attention has moved away from demolition and toward the design of an object meant to be valued for itself—a transition made easier, perhaps, because the references are to the world of nature rather than the world of man. At the same time the notion of indeterminacy remains central: even in the reduced Florida version the facade will "grow" and literally have a life of its own.

Venturi and Rauch's showroom

Top: SITE, Architects. Notch Showroom, 1977. Sacramento, California.
Bottom: SITE, Architects. Terrarium Showroom, 1978. South San Francisco, California.
Opposite: Tilt Showroom, 1978. Eudowood Mall, Towson, Maryland.

in Oxford Valley, Pennsylvania, has just been completed. Faithful to his own precepts, Venturi accepted the building as a "shed" requiring no substantial modifications to make it more impressive than its role requires. But as a shed it was a good subject for decoration. Venturi has made the walls out of porcelain-enamel panels with a large-scale pattern of flowers that is surprisingly pretty. Somewhere between Warhol and chintz, and with a little help from Matisse, the design seems meant only to please—and to please the full spectrum of taste. Like SITE's buildings it avoids substantive questions of architectural design, but at the same time it introduces a neglected resource.

Hardy Holzman Pfeiffer's administration building near Richmond, Virginia (photographed before completion), is the first of several segments which will ultimately make a long convex facade of glass block. As the plan indicates, the curve responds to the shape of the site and to the adjacent highway interchange; the irregular rear elevation opens to a wooded landscape. Windows the width of two glass blocks are arranged in a diamond pattern traversing the facade. A cornice of blue-gray ceramic tile adds decorative emphasis. Internally the plan provides an open office

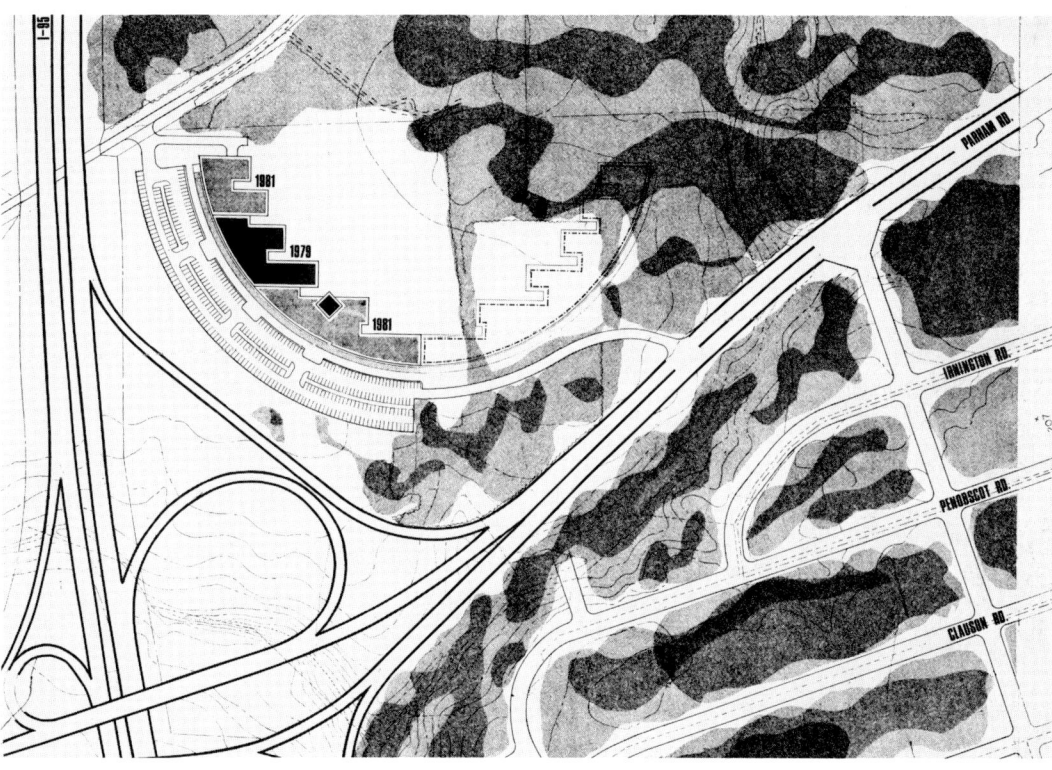

Above: Hardy Holzman Pfeiffer, Architects.
Plan for Corporate Headquarters, 1979.
Richmond, Virginia.
Opposite: Venturi and Rauch, Architects.
Showroom, 1979. Oxford Valley,
Pennsylvania.

landscape bisected by a curved "path" of color-differentiated carpet, paralleling the curve of the facade. Like Venturi's showroom, this building is somewhat more gentle than current moods might have been expected to produce.

What current moods might have been expected to produce is extra-architectural associations, and that is what all of the six architects commissioned to design new showroom facades have come up with. Perhaps by happenstance as much as by reasons of temperament, some of the projects exhibit other affinities.

Thus Stanley Tigerman and Robert A. M. Stern deal with a realignment of building types. Tigerman substitutes a house for a warehouse, but brings it up to warehouse scale. The source from which objects flow is made to look like a larger, more abundant version of the place in which they will be used and cherished, and the act of acquiring is tied to domesticity. For Stern it is not the domestic but the holy that suggests an appropriate configuration. Stern's facade is that of a temple. It recalls Henri Labrouste's reconstruction of the two temples of Hera at Paestum, particularly the famous section drawing which slices through a central line of columns and makes them look like a screen cut out of paper. Where Labrouste suggested that this temple had been decorated with trophies and inscriptions, Stern decorates with such modern trophies as television sets and tennis rackets. And where Labrouste meditated on how the Greeks must have used temples he thought were dedicated to Neptune, this temple presumably belongs to Jupiter Optimus Maximus—the Best and Greatest. Those born under the influence of his planet are joyful and happy, as the trophy-signs of a modern zodiac proclaim.

The projects by Charles Moore and Anthony Lumsden could scarcely be more different, but Moore borrows from the architecture of glass technology, with which Lumsden is so closely associated, the ubiquitous mirror. Moore's facade is a crystalline sculpture, a thick wall that fragments into a hundred facets, and which may not immediately be recognized as a representation of elephants carrying howdahs. The reflecting surface thus makes abstract an image Moore has borrowed and rearranged, namely, the angular elephants originally devised for San Francisco's almost forgotten World's Fair of 1939. The result manages to be at once abstract and figurative, as well as interesting, amiable, and zany. These qualities are in no way undermined by associations with ancient relief sculptures

Above: Henri Labrouste. Temple of Neptune [Hera I], Paestum. 1828–29 restoration of a building thought by Labrouste to have been used for public meetings and notices, and which he therefore called a "portique." From "The Architecture of the Ecole des Beaux-Arts," The Museum of Modern Art, New York, 1977
Opposite: Hardy Holzman Pfeiffer, Architects. Corporate Headquarters, 1979. Richmond, Virginia.

depicting Babylonian or Persian triumphs. Moore's symmetrical and triumphant procession of elephants does not include the actual spoils of war—which presumably are to be found inside the building.

Lumsden's project is perhaps the most astonishing of the six, and requires a word of explanation regarding its presentation. Although Lumsden began by exploring variations on the theme of curved glass canopies, similar to the rolling glass roofs he designed in 1973 for his Beverly Hills Hotel project, he left behind this almost straightforward use of glass-and-steel technology in favor of what he regards as a more purely sculptural conception. In his own comments (page 35) he declares an interest in exploring themes already tackled by SITE. Because his version makes use of the interpenetration of one form by another, he chose to make the model of solid wood, intending to emphasize sculptural solidity. This the model does, although at the expense of intelligibility, and so the wood model is supplemented by a more representational section model at larger scale. It is this section model that makes clear Lumsden's use of steel columns and trusses, together with the unexpected curves of a transparent glass roof in a configuration that seems almost improvised in its spontaneity. None of the refinements of a technologically directed architecture are aban-

Above: Bakewell and Weihe, Architects; Donald Macky, Sculptor. 1939. One of two 12-story-high Elephant Towers flanking the Portals of the Pacific, at the main entrance to the 1939 Golden Gate International Exposition, San Francisco, California.
Opposite page, top: Anthony Lumsden, Architect. Project for Beverly Hills Hotel, 1973. Los Angeles, California.
Five preliminary studies for glass canopies, Best Products showroom project, 1979.

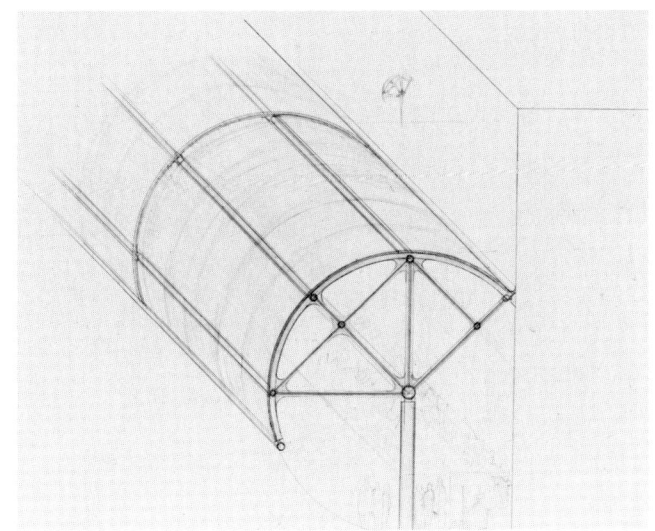
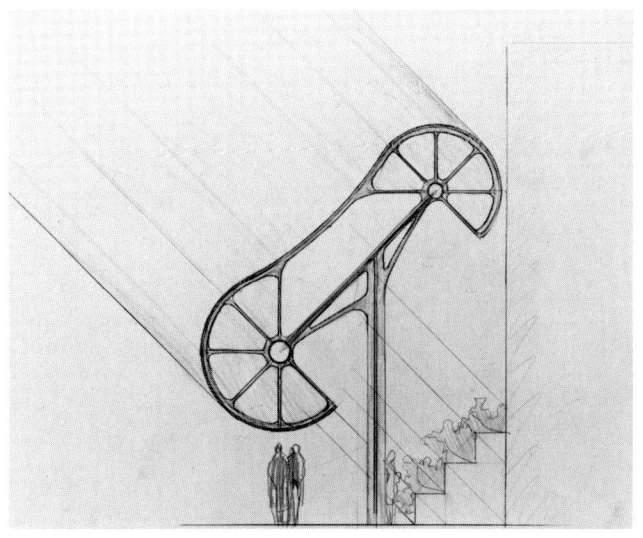
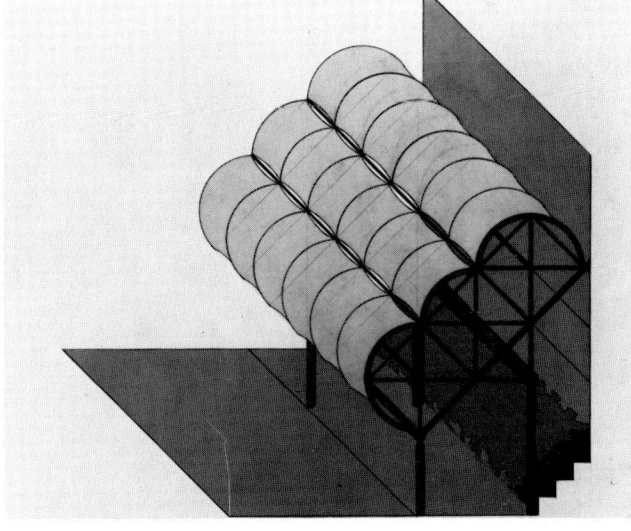
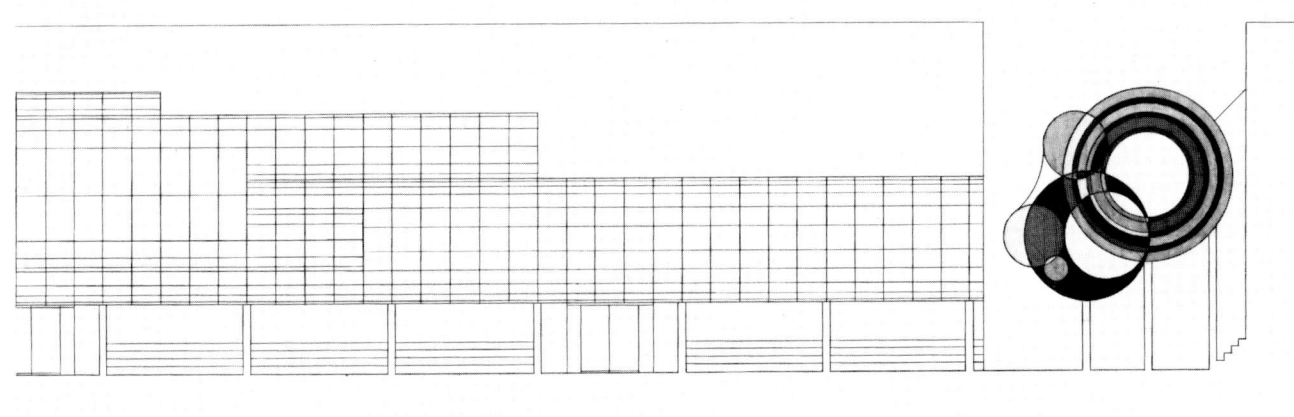
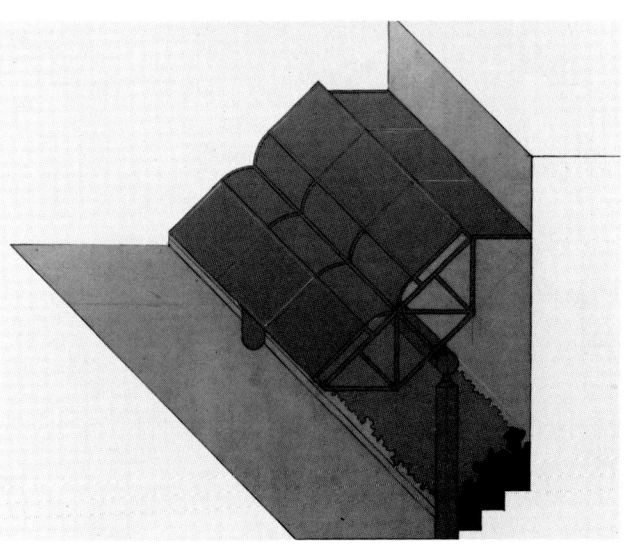

doned. Rather, its deliberate and predictable forms are placed at the service of what might be described as lyricism. The result is a work of considerable originality.

Michael Graves and Allan Greenberg approach the history of architecture in dead earnest. Greenberg regards the forms of classicism as alive and available, and his purpose in using them corresponds to the impulse that shaped them originally. Graves sees them as increasingly available, but for purposes of his own. Their different attitudes are also reflected in their understanding of the nature of the occasion: for Greenberg it is enough merely to apply a small, richly detailed portico, like a brooch, to the original building —which he is careful to leave visible. What is problematic about Greenberg's design is that it assumes something meant to evoke tradition and the "beautiful" can be taken seriously. Graves sees the portico or stoa as a building type best realized when it takes over the entire site, obliterating any building that happens to abut it. Less interested in the logic of the specific forms he is working with, Graves has produced a design that cannot be associated with a given style—except that the delicate stripes banding his columns (30' high and 8' in diameter) recall Art Deco *objets de luxe* along with ocean liners. One can imagine peddlers' stalls set up in the niches opposite the columns, and the association suggests that the natural evolution of Graves's stoa is to replace the showroom in function as well as in form. The design goes beyond the parameters of the problem, and yet it addresses itself forthrightly to the idea of a public place.

Tigerman, Stern, and Moore respond to the occasion with humor, but for Tigerman and Stern humor is simply another mode of moralizing. They cleave to what is essential in the tradition of orthodox modernism: the sermon. Sermons in plywood rather than steel, perhaps, but still sermons about the folly of our ways.

Lumsden, Graves, and Greenberg respond with sobriety, differing most of all in what they take seriously. Historicizing, which most modern architects do not take seriously, is by Greenberg completely and by Graves substantially removed from the realm of self-conscious irony. Coming from the opposite end of the spectrum, Lumsden deprives the engineer's technological style of its impersonal solemnity and puts it in the service of play—of form for its own sake—suggesting that the old glass bottle might yet serve new wine.

Michael Graves, Architect. Best Products showroom project, 1979. Perspective showing stoa extending beyond showroom building; and similar sheltered walk paralleling highway.

Stanley Tigerman

The Best Home of All

Since World War II (an unbelievable 35 years ago!) the United States of America has quietly been nurturing a typological evolution as homespun as John Wayne—the suburban house. The objecthood of this form is as solidly American as Frank Lloyd Wright—embracing the hip roof (replete with overhangs), the corner window and the wing wall (both of which represent vestiges of Wright's breakup of the foursquare, symmetrically axial, 19th-century aristocratic European box).

    Now the suburban house has an identity of scale as solidly real as the brick (Mies van der Rohe once said that "the brick is made to fit the hand"). By now, almost the entire recent generation-come-of-age has experienced the suburban context—the "Hilbersheimer Tee-Plan" brought into being in all of this continent's Levittized environments. Iconographically, the suburban house is as American as television (God knows, all its aerials search-and-sweep the sky like so many centipedal antennae). Only one very small, alien element clouds the otherwise clear azure dome over suburban America—the uneuphemized, uncleansed, naked capitalist without any emperor's clothes at all—the commercial-strip shopping center.

    And so it was that the Best search for a new home began. Really, they just had to find a comfortable place—one that could kind of nuzzle up to its little friends, so that when they

came out to shop it would be as if they had never left home. If they drove to the store, why, they could just park their car right on the front lawn. The Best mailbox would be just like their very own, only four times as big. The garage door would be partially open, just like their own broken one, and the front door would be invitingly open as well, revealing an American-dream-come-true-at-last... A 22' tall beckoning fair one as American and as wonderfully wholesome as Mary Tyler Moore. From the highway, their Best new home would settle contextual arguments once and for all, and you would never even really notice that each front step was 32" high, that the front door was 12' wide x 26'8" high, that the downspouts were 16" in diameter, that each brick was 15" high x 32" long (with 1½" mortar joints), and that you would walk right by the areawell-as-bench right into the basement window-as-door.

Nearly the Best part of all was the four seasons. Halloween would feature a 10' black cat peering from behind the draped living-room window, with 20' corn shocks on the lawn and a grinning 8' jack-o'-lantern sitting right there on the front stoop. At Christmastime 16" lights would be strung around the picture window revealing a 25' Christmas tree—and on the roof, a 25' Santa, sleigh, and reindeer. Easter would find 4' tall bunny-rabbits hopping up and down on the lawn searching for colorful 12" Easter eggs hidden between the cars. But the Best season of all would be the Fourth of July. A 24' American flag would join the rest of the neighboring flags in celebrating America's birthday. Red and white striped bunting would surround the garage door, and a 16' wide x 32' long x 10' high picnic table would be found at rest in the driveway, with a 12' high Weber grill nearby.

Of course, the very Best thing about their new home lay in its neighborliness, insofar as they had finally found an American symbol right there where they least expected it—at home in the suburban United States of America—and all the snotty bastards in the urban United States were simply green with envy.

The basic building is shown in elevation at the top.
Below, from left to right, it is shown with seasonal changes for Halloween, Christmas, Easter, and the Fourth of July.

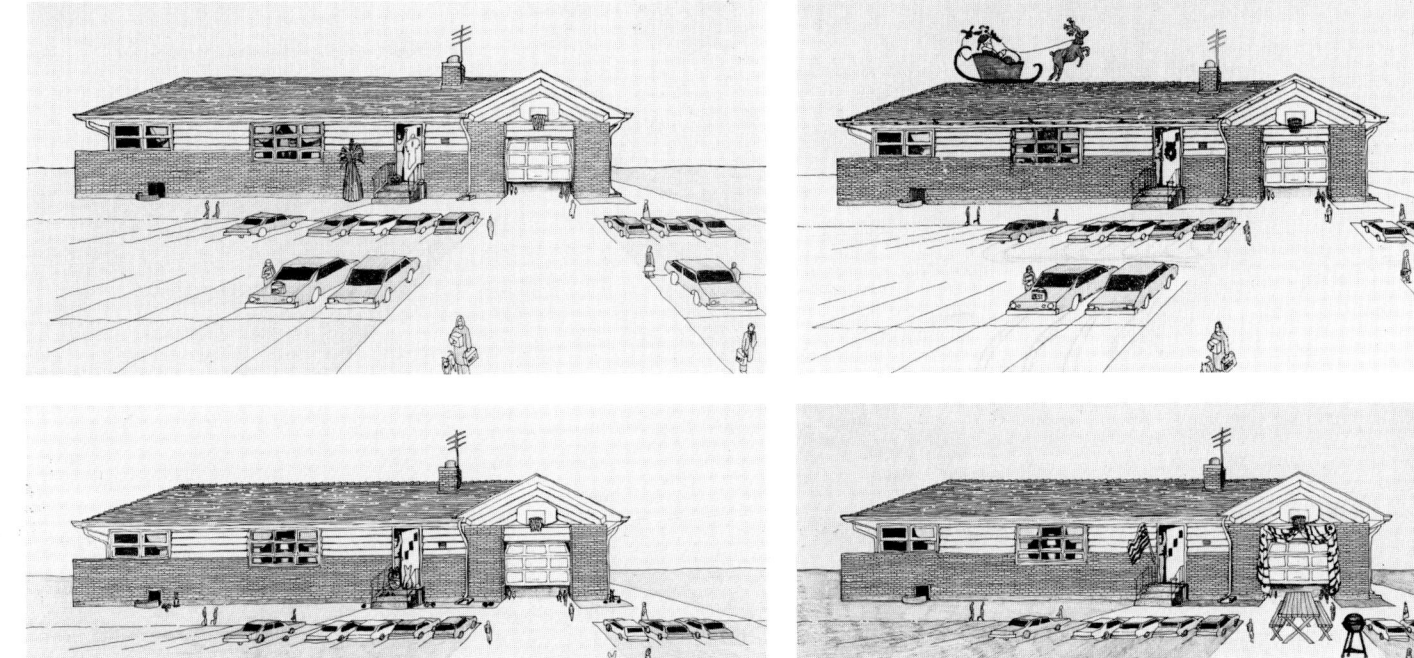

Robert A. M. Stern

Gavin Macrae-Gibson, assistant-in-charge; model by John Ike and Mark Albert; perspective by Gavin Macrae-Gibson and Charles Warren

The Earth, the Temple, and the Goods.

The standard Best Products building is a box whose purpose is to supply the objects that are demanded by and in part define the lives of those who live out a version of the American Dream—a version in which material possessions, once the objects of religious sacrifice, now serve to mark out rituals of daily life. To a considerable extent our household goods have become our household gods; our markets, temples of consumerism. In designing a facade for Best, we have undertaken to tell the story of this transformation of values in a witty way, and to describe the cycle of life to which it bears witness.

It has been observed that shopping has become a cultural act for many Americans. For this reason the temple front, with its widely recognized associations in high culture, seems appropriate. The bold scale of the pediment silhouetted against the sky, and of the stoa-arcade, gives the showroom enough "skyline" and enough "mass" to be seen by motorists bowling along the highway. The attention of the motorist is first held by the letters within the pediment, which have replaced the sculpture of antiquity, while at closer range the introduction of columnlike cutouts within the arcade brings the scale down to one that is sympathetic to the parked car and the pedestrian.

The columns have been squashed by the great weight of the pediment and record the changes that have taken place in the anatomy of the temple; yet they can also be read as table-legs, the canopies as table-tops, supporting the goods as if in a residential setting. The gold color refers to the sacrificial instruments of archaic rites, while suggesting the affluence of contemporary American society. The stoa-arcade and its heroically scaled metopes are the guardians of the temple, with its treasures within, standing upright, braced with outstretched arms against the enormous space of the parking lot.

The facade is intended to be read in a number of specific ways. The classical language transforms the catalog showroom into a temple of consumerism; the columns of the stoa-arcade carry out the historical theme of consumerism and support metopes whose silhouetted images depict typical products sold by Best. The placement of each metope-image corresponds to the approximate location of the product depicted in the showroom; at the same time the arrangement of the metopes on the facade can be read from left to right documenting an idealized cycle of contemporary life: courtship leading to engagement; marriage with its wedding gifts and attendant photographically recorded hoopla; the wedding trip followed by the routine of married life, with hours spent watching television; the passage of time leading to childbirth and the repetition of the cycle.

The front door penetrates the cycle in the center. What was the opening in the inside wall of the temple becomes solid and comes forward, and the column that would have stood in front of it becomes the void through which the portal is entered. The huge void column "supports" the letter "T" above, and is thus related to the smaller void columns on either side, but at the scale of the landscape rather than at the scale of the cars in the parking lot. The column beyond the silhouette is the last vestige of the real columns that once existed, but it is made of glass, the material of museum cases, and it is through this object that the temple with its affordable treasures is entered.

The facade is to be built of porcelain-enameled-steel and anodized-aluminum panels, the former assembled in such a way as to suggest the rusticated masonry of the enclosing cella walls of traditional temples, the latter serving as the cladding of the elements in the stoa-arcade, including the metopes that carry out the program of narrative decoration.

In the drawing, a larger cycle of time is superimposed on the life-cycle portrayed in the facade. The catalog showroom is shown in its typical setting along a roadside strip, taking a position in relation to the natural landscape and to the present man-made and man-manipulated environment. The siting of the Best temple, like that of examples from ancient Greece, tells a story of men and the forces of nature, of hubris, and of reverence for things as they are.

Charles Moore
with Jim Winkler and Robert Flock of the Urban Innovations Group, Los Angeles

The distant ancestors of these 12 guardian elephants may have trumpeted through the Asian temple, but their immediate forebears emerged radiantly from the prismatic illuminated towers that turned the San Francisco Fair in 1939 into ephemeral magic. Architects Bakewell and Weihe and sculptor Donald Macky brought the parent elephants forth from solid (though pastel) plinths. For me there is particular aerial wonder in their trunks—long, leaning, inverted obelisks resting on smaller plinths—or even their howdahs, with ambiguous recollections of Oriental luxury and the cooling towers of an air-conditioning system.

All we did was bring the elephants off the towers, multiply them, and cover them with reflective porcelain enamel, the better to make connections with the shopping center around.

Why elephants, instead of, say, zebras or giraffes or donkeys or tigers? Well, the Mogul emperor Akbar and his whole dynasty favored elephants, and they had a superior grasp of these matters. Why Macky's elephants? Because surely a really good thing has the right to return to the planet after forty years' absence.

Anthony Lumsden

Above: Wood model showing front elevation of masonry facade and glass canopy. Opposite page: Side view.

The showroom box is slightly modified, its facade being expressed as an opaque plane articulated by recesses at the corners, which serve as entrances. A curved umbrella enclosure replaces the standard rectilinear canopy. It is angled in plan in relation to the box. Planters and steps are placed at one corner of the showroom and adjacent to the projected end of the glass umbrella. This develops a potential enclosed space adjacent to the entry. It could be used to display outdoor items, or operate as a flower/plant/landscape shop, or as a coffee shop with a palm-court environment. Materials are brick, metal, and glass. Color would depend on the physical context of the showroom. The logo is intended to be inflated and flown above the building.

The curved cyma recta–cyma reversa form of the canopy is geometrically constructed from four quarters of a circle, alternately reversed. The section of the canopy is revealed, as if extruded, adjacent to the corner entrances, and is expressed on the elevation by the canopy's apparent penetration of the brick wall. The resulting elevation approximates the "de-architecturized" facade by SITE for Best's Houston showroom. The planters terminate in formalized concave erosion, recalling the "de-architecturization" of the entrance in the Best Baltimore showroom. The canopy and planters modify the isolation of the showroom box, changing its form and reducing its scale.

The Best showroom project continues to investigate an architectural vocabulary I have used for several years: the membrane aesthetic; the extruded facade; intersecting forms; and reversed curves. In this project destruction of the box is intended without identifying with inversion and entropy as generative resources.

Above: Wood model showing side view of masonry facade and glass canopy.
Below and far right: Section model showing steel structure and transparent glass roof.

Allan Greenberg
model by Richard Wies and Suzanne Butolph

Colonnades and arcades are traditional architectural forms that have been used, since antiquity, to define shopping precincts and other places for people to gather. The simple canopies used by contemporary retail outlets are impoverished versions of these ancient prototypes. A similar impoverishment affects the overall design of many shopping centers, despite the important role of these complexes in the physical organization of suburban and rural communities.

This proposal for a Best showroom uses the firm's basic prototype building. Across the facade, facing parking and access route, is a colonnade. At its center an arch articulates the main entrance and also ensures the building's imageability from a distance. If the shopping complex has a number of stores, the colonnade can be extended to encompass exterior and interior malls so as to create a unified composition.

The classical language of architecture simplifies the problem of providing shelter from the elements and physical identity for the retail outlet by using beautiful architectural forms that have been honed to physical perfection by the experience of centuries. Contrary to recent dogma, the classical tradition is not dead, and its forms are neither overly expensive nor impractical. The "Tuscan" order used in this project is appropriate for retail buildings, which lack the symbolic and civic connotations of public and religious buildings, but are more important than purely utilitarian structures such as warehouses or barns. The moldings, floor pattern, entryway details, and color provide visual enrichment, which is supplemented by the textures of the natural materials. The materials proposed for the Best colonnade are Roman brick for the wall, which is whitewashed under the colonnade; limestone for pedestals, columns, and wainscot; marble and slate for plinth and floor; and bronze and marble for the entryways.

By following the example of the past and by using the forms and meanings of classical architecture, we can make our shopping precincts and their buildings richer and more coherent works of architecture that will assume their rightful places in the American landscape.

Michael Graves

In considering the city in terms of its patterns of use, the idea of commerce becomes distinguished from other primary urban activities. One recognizes that commerce has the formal and social capacity to bind and synthesize a variety of other city activities. While the commercial aspects of the city have taken various forms depending on their context, one feels that they themselves are very strong contributors to determining that context.

There appear to be three primary types of commercial organization, which could be loosely defined as: one, the field, forum, or agora; two, the street; and three, the galleria, a form closely related to the street. In the first instance, the Greek stoa, occurring within the open field or agora, can be seen as distinctly different from the more continuous city grid. The stoa building can describe the edge of the field while its open side forms a continuous portico available to the adjacent agora. In the example of the urban grid of streets, the intensity of the grid is not understood as an open field, as in the former example, but as a continuous linear network. The third example, the galleria, is closely related to the street but takes its primary character from subdividing the Cartesian grid and allowing internal passage that is often covered. The single most important aspect of all of these types is also the most favorable form for shopping, that is, a linear progression. We tend to organize our pattern of

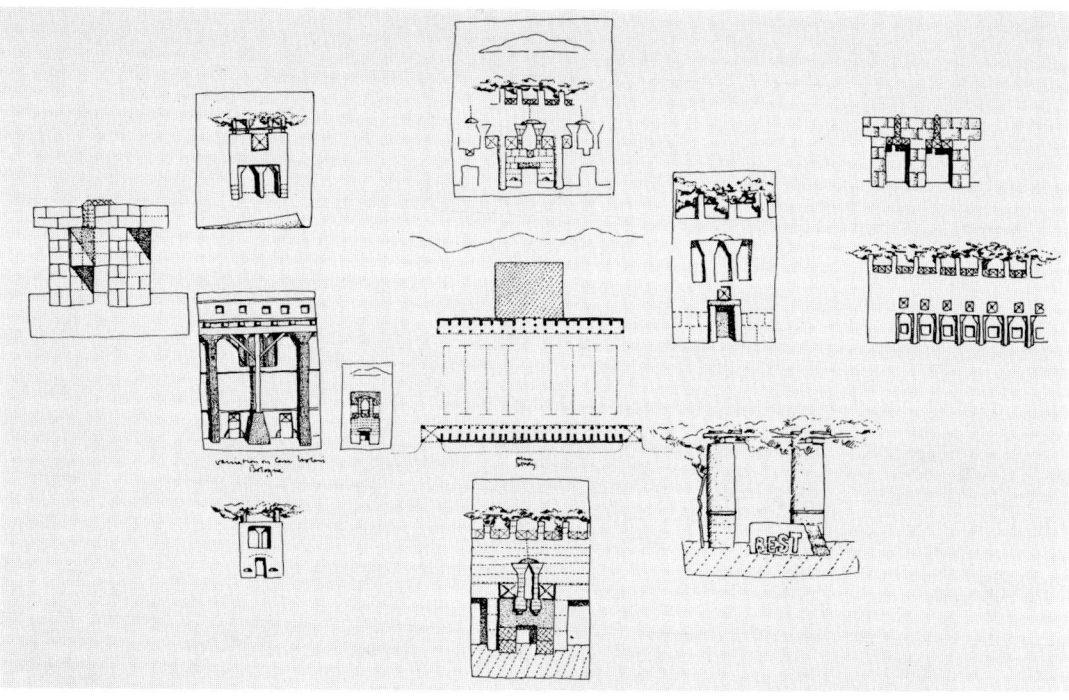

This page: Preliminary studies and final site plan.
Opposite page, top: Elevation drawing showing portico same length as building; model shows it extended beyond building.

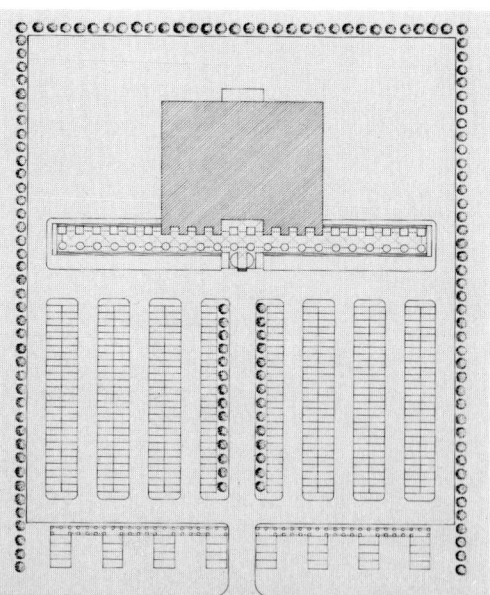

shopping according to our ability to examine the goods at hand, and therefore close contact with the elements offered for trade is best understood in a linear progression whether one is examining the pattern of trade in the stoa, the street, or the galleria.

However, as we consider the shopping districts that occur in the extended city, namely its fringes, strips, and suburbs, we discover an amalgam of these types contained in one. When commercialism requires more parking than is available to any single building, the tendency has of course been to group a number of complementary commercial activities in larger centers of shopping. The dominant type has been a quasi-rectangular ring with parking on the outside of the ring, entrance to the various commercial elements on the inside of the ring, and what has to be regarded as a somewhat residual but extensive piece of turf at the center.

In this pattern, we find ourselves, after having parked the car, facing the back sides of buildings with passages to the center within. This ambiguous, honorific center provides access to the actual fronts of the commercial line. In other words, the organization has turned in on itself in order to suggest the cohesion of the internal shopping ring. One realizes that this is caused by simple geometry, where one understands the internal order by virtue of its visual comprehension while one would not be able to understand the entire complex from any one of its external sides. Because of the ambiguities of front and back, parking to central mall, etc., this pattern continues to be thought of as some sort of unresolved formal dilemma.

To overcome this geometric curiosity, there has been a tendency to identify the major or larger commercial entities as special and to allow them primary access from parking, thereby subverting the organizational comprehension that the center mall once held. It is only after passing through the larger individual shopping facilities that we gain access to the center of the whole. The further development of this type is now seen as an attempt to make the center more desirable than in its former residual character by enclosing it as a galleria or skylit line in order to restore the centrality of the place and offer more comfortable accommodations. The net result of this development has been a continual erosion of the street or highway so that one is now offered only the view of enormous parking fields with the concentration of shopping centers growing from their midst.

One imagines that this tendency could be subverted if one were to reverse the present pattern of the shopping center and once and for all admit the presence of the car as a significant and symbolic fact of the suburb, not to glorify it but to acknowledge its significance. If one were to turn the shopping center inside out and park in the agora or "mall" and shop at its edge, one would retain the benefit of linear shopping patterns, reduce the present waste caused by our increasing honorific and meaningless centers (non-centers), and restore to the street some legibility. In our proposal for the Best Products building, we have extended the dimension of the facade with a covered pergola which allows smaller merchants to be housed on that route, or allows the primary tenant, Best, to offer that space to more loosely defined trade activities such as flea markets or antique fairs. Similar activity is structured along the street; pavilions with signage announce the presence of the primary tenant and allow certain selling functions to separate quite naturally from the larger warehouse enclosure of Best.

The parallel lines of shopping, one at the street and one extending the face of the Best building, have the potential to ring the site if it is thought desirable to have more rentable space. It is felt that this scheme retains the historical and physical requirements of linear shopping and yet does not pretend to be anything more than it is.

Trustees of
The Museum of Modern Art

William S. Paley
Chairman of the Board

Gardner Cowles
Mrs. Bliss Parkinson
David Rockefeller
Vice Chairmen

Mrs. John D. Rockefeller 3rd
President

Mrs. Frank Y. Larkin
Donald B. Marron
John Parkinson III
Vice Presidents

John Parkinson III
Treasurer

Mrs. L. vA. Auchincloss
Edward Larrabee Barnes
Alfred H. Barr, Jr.*
Mrs. Armand P. Bartos
Gordon Bunshaft
Shirley C. Burden
William A. M. Burden
Thomas S. Carroll
Frank T. Cary
Ivan Chermayeff
Mrs. C. Douglas Dillon*
Gianluigi Gabetti
Paul Gottlieb
George Heard Hamilton
Wallace K. Harrison*
William A. Hewitt
Mrs. Walter Hochschild*
Mrs. John R. Jakobson
Philip Johnson
Ronald S. Lauder
John L. Loeb
Ranald H. Macdonald*
Mrs. G. Macculloch Miller*

J. Irwin Miller*
S. I. Newhouse, Jr.
Richard E. Oldenburg
Peter G. Peterson
Gifford Phillips
Mrs. Albrecht Saalfield
Mrs. Wolfgang Schoenborn*
Martin E. Segal
Mrs. Bertram Smith
Mrs. Alfred R. Stern
Mrs. Donald B. Straus
Walter N. Thayer
R. L. B. Tobin
Edward M. M. Warburg*
Mrs. Clifton R. Wharton, Jr.
Monroe Wheeler*
John Hay Whitney*

*Honorary Trustee

Ex Officio

Edward I. Koch
Mayor of the City of New York

Harrison J. Goldin
Comptroller of the City of New York

Photo Credits

Cover, Jim Winkler; pp. 8, 9, 10, 11, 12, 13, courtesy SITE; p. 14, courtesy Venturi and Rauch; p. 16, Dennis McWaters; p. 17, J.-E. Bulloz/MoMA; p. 18, The Bettman Archive, Inc.; pp. 26, 27, 31, 34, 35, 36, 37, 39, 40/41, 43, 44, 45, Wolfgang Hoyt/ESTO; pp. 32/33, Marvin Rand.